The Normandy Mulberry Harbours

THE PITKIN GUIDE

MULBERRY HARBOUR A (AMERICAN)

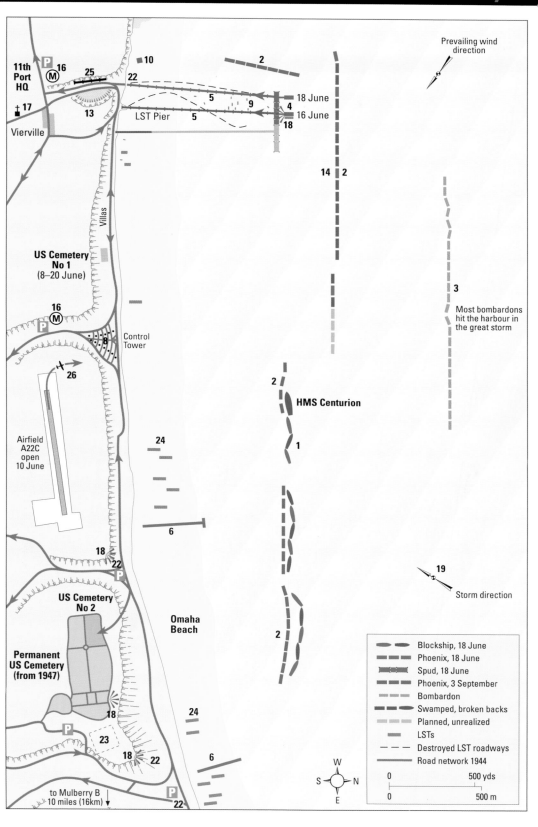

Prevailing wind direction

11th Port HQ

P **16** (M) **25** **22** **10** **2**

17 **13** **5** **9** **4** 18 June

Vierville

LST Pier **5** **16** June **18**

14 **2**

Villas

US Cemetery No 1 (8–20 June)

3

Most bombardons hit the harbour in the great storm

P (M) **16**

8 Control Tower

26

2

HMS Centurion

Airfield A22C open 10 June

1

24

6

19

Storm direction

18 **22** P

2

US Cemetery No 2

Permanent US Cemetery (from 1947)

Omaha Beach

18

P

23

24

18 **22**

6

to Mulberry B 10 miles (16km)

22 P

W

S — N

E

0 — 500 yds

0 — 500 m

Legend:
- Blockship, 18 June
- Phoenix, 18 June
- Spud, 18 June
- Phoenix, 3 September
- Bombardon
- Swamped, broken backs
- Planned, unrealized
- LSTs
- Destroyed LST roadways
- Road network 1944

'There was a vast sense of relief and pride in the hearts of the Mulberry men. It had been a race against time, but as one looked out over the shimmering water and the structures, it seemed clear that the Germans were now too late. Nothing could stop the swelling strength of our forces now pouring over the bouncing steel roadway to shore. For the first time it really seemed possible that the war could be won.'
COMMANDER ALFRED STANFORD,
FORCE MULBERRY

Two British Bedford trucks, which have come across the Channel on Fairy, are waiting to leave. The powerful platform capstan is by the hexagonal rolls of buffer matting. Moored beyond the two trucks are a Mulberry tug and a fishing boat from Grandcamp, which will end up smashed under buffer pontoon no. 432; perhaps it has provided the men with fish. Bundles of sticks are used as simple buffers to protect ships and craft alongside the beechwood fenders of the spud pier.

BELOW: Nearly all of the spud piers were made in Scotland. Part ship, part elevator, the oblong floating steel hull, rises and falls with the 23-ft (7-m) tide, guided by cables strung over the tops of the spud legs. The winches keep the platform 6ins (15cm) above its free-floating level, pressing its pointed, splayed feet into the sand; it is perfectly stable without anchors, fulfilling Churchill's original criteria (see page 1). In years to come oil rigs will be developed using the same principles as spud piers, and 'roll on, roll off' Channel ferries from LSTs. As can be seen from the legs, it is low tide: 20ft (6m). In this composite photograph the western spuds (visible on page 2) have been reconstructed to give a sense of scale. Compare this to the apparent size of the LST pierhead in Mulberry B (page 13, no. 24).

Arromanches

It is 80 days later – Sunday 3 September; quiet and sunny. The battles in Normandy have been fought and won. Paris and Rouen are now liberated, Lyon today and Antwerp tomorrow. But next Tuesday, beginning at 1754 hours, Le Havre, just 35 miles (55km) away, will be obliterated with the loss of over 2,000 civilian lives. Arromanches, however, is fortunate; apart from the demolition of houses on D-Day for road access by Royal Engineers around the present car park and museum site, the village at the heart of these titanic movements of material has suffered much disturbance but little damage.

A tank-transporter (1) is waiting where coaches disembark today. The villa in the foreground (2) overlooking the village is still very prominent; the gun bunker to its left (3), partly concealed in the grass, is today topped by a Sherman tank. A fuel line (4) comes in parallel to the eastern central stores roadway (5) and runs up the hill to a vast cargo transfer area (see map, no. 8) where vehicles can refuel. The roadway itself comes to the stone slope east of the present museum.

Just beyond the roof line of the villa, the western central embarkation roadway (6) comes in to a breach (7) visible in the massive anti-tank wall next to the bunker on the lookout point jutting out to sea; today a telescope is positioned on it. The wall borders the present car park and blocks off the stone hards used by fishing boats in times past.

Of Ducks and Swiss Rolls

At the western end of the cleared ground is the Hotel de la Marine. Beyond it the western barge pier (8) comes in, and along the foreshore marked by holiday villas built in the 1850s, we can just make out the DUKW entrance, today apparently quiet. Ducks, operating 24 hours a day, their crews driving in relays, have handled more cargo than the stores piers. As a result the engines are beginning to wear out. The Royal Engineers carved a road west up the hill (9) behind the cliffs of Tracy sur Mer; the road is still very evident today. The village is straddled by large transfer and handling depots for the lorries and Ducks coming ashore here and east towards Asnelles (see map). Where the cliff line begins we can see the 'Swiss Roll' (10), a 2,000-ft (600-m) experimental floating roadway made of wooden planks held together with steel cables (see page 7). Its load limit is equivalent to a three-ton lorry, and it is used for disembarking naval personnel. A vehicle driven along the Swiss Roll out of a landing craft raises hinged wooden sides by displacement. Today the roadway appears to be partially sunk.

The western arm of the breakwater (11), reinforced with Phoenixes from Mulberry A, abuts a rubble promontory. A quarry has been created here to enable barges to dump rubble around the breakwaters as an anti-scour protection to stop the powerful currents pushing between the caissons and scooping away the sand under the ends, weakening and breaking them. At the same time beach sand is being pumped into some of the caissons to increase their resistance to wave action.

In the traditional method, a beached LST would take two hours to discharge and then wait up to ten hours to refloat on the incoming tide. But at 1830 hours on 16 June, LST 543 returns to the UK, arriving at Southampton for reloading the following morning, some 12 hours later. Meanwhile, there is a conference on board the flagship USS *Augusta* on how to enlarge and prolong the use of the Mulberry facilities into the winter. Next day, on 18 June, LST 543 empties its load a second time at the pierhead. By then 11 LSTs have docked here, taking an average of 64 minutes each. Morale has never been so high. And for 19 June, the first full day of operation of both LST piers together, the weather is forecast 'fair to cloudy, little change'.

The three roadways, in different stages of readiness, reach towards us. One bridge 'train' is being manoeuvred into position by two motor launches. Holiday villas, some still there today, mark the line of the coastal road, widened by US engineers. Bodies from the D-Day assault were still floating in on the beach. Before the Vierville valley, the violence of the naval gunnery there has churned up the chalky limestone, making the bluff look white.

The easternmost roadway (see page 6) for a 25-ton load limit consists as yet of only two 'trains' and work there has been stopped to make up the central roadway with its sections. The thin, brittle concrete floats keep failing, and six bridge trains have already been lost mid-Channel (40 per cent will eventually be lost). The roadways are shortened by 480ft (150m), and the eastern roadway cannibalized to complete the other, originally destined for a 40-ton limit. The attack on Cherbourg urgently requires heavy material. Twenty 38-ton tanks will, later this evening, make a trial run on the 25-ton load limit (see sign at road junction on platform below); after negotiating the unravelled mats on the buffer, the tanks, carefully spaced out, gingerly take to the roadway. As they slump down to their skirts, the onlooking British think of their disastrous 'Swiss Roll' experiments in which 10-ton trucks had seemed to 'walk on water' on a floating boardwalk – before sagging to a stop and making an undignified exit beneath the waves (see page 9, no. 10). Today, however, all the tanks make it ashore – just.

BELOW: Brotherly banter about the Limey-made equipment was hardly surprising, it having been delivered without manuals just two weeks before D-Day. The Americans had therefore unilaterally set up a full-scale practice run. On 24 May, at Peel Bank, Isle of Wight, a loaded British LST slid up the buffer, as seen here.

Under the horrified eyes of all the assembled admirals and generals, it was found that not only could the bow doors not be opened but, once the base of the bow doors had been trimmed with oxyacetylene torches, tracked vehicles and tanks slithered down off the wet steel back into the ship. Heavy wooden mats (see page 7) were prepared to give some grip, but the incident, on the very day it was announced that many Phoenixes were stuck on the sea bed off Selsey, underlined the experimental and hurried nature of every aspect of Mulberry.

Jeeps and trucks begin rolling off one by one; several are on the roadway already. The lead 2.5-ton GMC truck has to negotiate the tight turn between the white painted guidelines. A man standing on the parapet (see page 7) bellows at the driver through a bullhorn. With the upper deck also cleared the LST will be empty of its 78 vehicles in just 38 minutes and is ordered to leave at 1800 hours to make way for the next LST, and to pick up its next load. The record time for emptying an LST of its vehicles, realized at Mulberry B in July, was just 18 minutes.

The immediate task is to start unrolling the 1,000-ft (300-m) long anchor wires to secure the roadway floats via the waiting 'Slug' in the sea close to the roadway (see pages 6–7): the bulky spools of cable can be seen with the Mulberry men sitting on them. Only one in six floats is as yet secure; the task does not seem so important with such a prolonged spell of fine weather predicted. But the visiting British, with their long experience of Channel waters, do not like the look of it, or the one-foot (30-cm) freeboard on the Phoenixes, with the gathering spring tide on the way. The loaded Liberty ship only needs a 24-ft (8-m) draught. As the roadways have been shortened to save on floats, the Phoenixes are now positioned unnecessarily far out.

Of Spuds, Slugs and Detached Moles

Between the eastern entrance (12) and the northern entrance (13) stretches the 'Detached Mole', most of which survives today, being bedded on rock and not subject to 'scour'. In the sky, cables are suspended under the occasional token barrage balloon to discourage low-flying German aircraft – that fail to make an appearance.

A gigantic floating crane (14), so large it was able to shift other cranes, tanks, bulldozers and similar heavy equipment onto pierheads, stands out to the left of the three spud platforms of the L-shaped munitions pier. The half-mile (800-metre) line of seven spud piers (15) and their concrete extension platforms and bridging is the single most striking feature of the harbour, allowing seven Liberty ships moored bow to stern to discharge at the same time. From 7 July a traffic flow is established whereby empty lorries could drive up the western central roadway and return, loaded, down the eastern central roadway.

Closer to the spuds are 'Slugs' (Surf Landing Under Girder boats) moored in pairs, and 'erection tanks' (16). The 20ft- (6m-) long Slugs look like weaving shuttles and threaded the 1,000ft- (300m-) long anchor cables for the roadway floats or 'Beetles'; they had to be capable of passing under the roadways between the floats while paying out the cables. The Slugs, no longer needed, are parked in the area of calmest water. One can be seen next to the Mulberry A roadway on pages 6–7, being made ready to receive the cable.

Discarded 19-ton concrete floats (17) today lie on the beach between the two roadways, where they were left before the storm (19–21 June). When the roadways either side were completed, the tanks and floats were trapped there and never removed.

Of Beetles, Bombardons and Erection Tanks

Further west lies an 850-ton concrete extension pontoon (18). The extension pontoon for the second LST pierhead at Vierville still lies on the beach there, a distant echo of the existence of two Mulberries. These pontoons are the same width (60ft/18m) as the spud pier, adding length (80ft/24m) to the pierhead to accommodate a Liberty ship, and providing turning space for vehicles. They have flared sides and swim ends to make them easy to tow; inside there are 18 compartments, one of them for living accommodation. They have been made strong enough for heavy lorries, but not to withstand berthing shocks.

Moored among the Slugs are seven steel erection tanks (19); two are close to shore. These have been used to help line up the bridge spans by being filled with water under the 'bow' of the incoming towed bridge 'train' of six 80-ft (24-m) sections. Buoys (20) mark off the area closed to all boats.

Note that it is possible to distinguish between the fragile 19-ton concrete Beetle slumped on the sand (21), and the sturdier 16-ton metal Beetles (22) standing on adjustable spud legs. Only eight or nine concrete floats lie on the sandy beach under each roadway. The concrete floats had caused a lot of trouble: 20,000 tons of steel and huge amounts of desperately needed docking space had been wasted on the Bombardons (all were scrapped after the great storm) yet most of the floats had been manufactured in one-inch (3-cm) brittle concrete to save on 5,000 tons of steel. After the storm, concrete Beetles were no longer used; those in position were replaced by steel floats with spuds.

'With a roar, the first vehicle [a DUKW] instantly emerged [see back cover] and went up the ramp of the buffer pontoon, and then turned into the roadway. With but a brief grin at the spontaneous ripple of applause from the crowd on the Lobnitz pier, the driver set off down the steel tracks toward shore at 15 miles an hour as though he had been doing this just every day of his life …

The dream of Mulberry actually worked. Grim-faced generals … suddenly fell to slapping the nearest navy man on the back. There was cocky talk with the Brits present about American drive and general superiority. Mulberry B is days behind A, and ashore the British Army was up against German armor in strength that blocked the seizure of Caen. The American forces … were streaming [up] the Cotentin peninsula. There was talk of capturing Cherbourg in ten days: the US Mulberry was a reality.'

ALFRED STANFORD, DEPUTY COMMANDER
MULBERRY A, *FORCE MULBERRY*

BELOW: Photograph taken on Susie's southern bridge. All work stops as the navy men and Seabees gather before the 14-ft (4-m) wide bow doors at the eastern end of platform 516 (Fairy) where two sea tugs are moored. In the history of warfare this is a unique moment. At the foot of the spud winching housing below, three men stand together looking at the LST. Dick Lane, the LST pharmacist's mate; in the middle (wearing a woollen cap) motor machinist's mate Roy Carter; and, on Roy Carter's right, is Marvin Zimmermann, watertender. Note that the spud pier is riveted, whereas the LST is welded — which saved on steel and time.

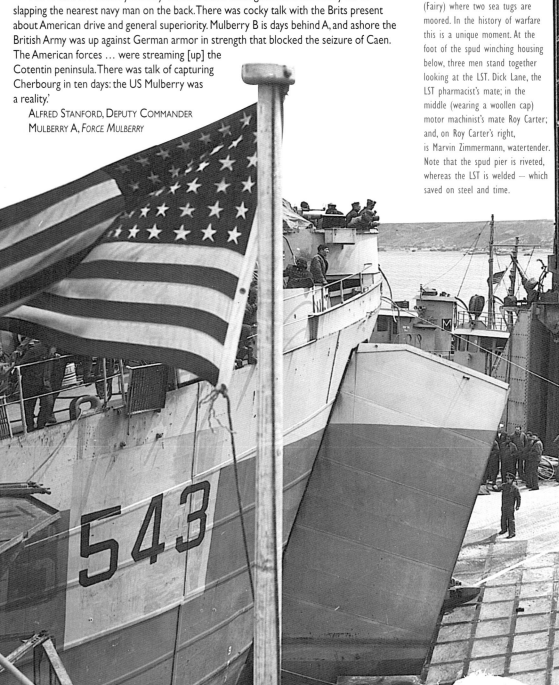

Of Gooseberries, and Rhinos and Baileys on the flanks

The Gooseberry (23) has by now been double-banked with Phoenixes for extra protection against the coming autumn, as has been done at Mulberry A. Looking to the east we can see a white hospital ship (24) berthed at the LST pier to receive the wounded. The LST roadway, opened on 19 July, came in at the eastern end of the headland to a Bailey bridge: today a plaque by the beach marks the site. (A Bailey bridge can be visited at Pegasus Bridge, north of Caen, where many were once used.) Two bridging 'trains', 16 and 13 sections long (25), are beached alongside the LST roadway, a reserve originally destined for Mulberry A; although 40 per cent of roadways were lost, 25 per cent had been made surplus to the requirements of the two harbours, leaving spares in the eventuality of storms to come. At the seaward end of these spare 'trains' we can see the western entrance with its 'boat camber' (26). The entrance is flanked by six Phoenixes to the west, originally destined for Mulberry A, and six more to make a shelter for smaller craft (see map): only one today retains its Bofors anti-aircraft gun-platform. At the point where the eastern arm reaches the shore looms the rectangular profile of the wrecked sanatorium at Le Hamel (27), now demolished, and the gun tower at Asnelles, which served as a useful landmark for positioning the eastern breakwater. It also marks the beginning of the British landing beach known as Gold (28). A Rhino pontoon causeway runs in from the sea. The headland – near the site of the present cinema – is littered with debris and barbed wire.

While the conception and production of the Mulberries was entirely British, the decision to go for it (made at Quebec, 10–24 August 1943), the design of the Phoenix caissons, the towing operations and the assembly on each side of the Channel were shared by the British and Americans. Twenty-two blockships were American.

Delays, secrecy and the labyrinthine chains of command led to friction. The Americans could not believe the British were so blithely optimistic about the whole thing. But it also led to friendships and a healthy sense of competition at lower levels of command, which pushed the Americans to take great pride in being the first to put into operation their LST pier. Informal exchanges of Royal Navy pink gin for American beef helped things along.

Under the manic drive of Captain A. Dayton Clark, USN commander of Mulberry A which was built off Omaha Beach, all was ready on the 'far shore' three days ahead of schedule. A second LST pier would open alongside two days later. In ensuring that the war photographers were out in force to record this historic moment, the US authorities have allowed us to see exactly how the LST piers worked.

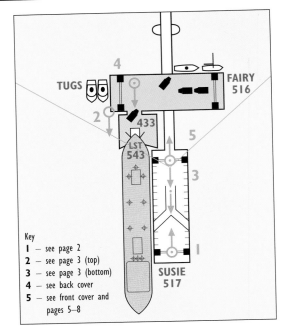

Key
1 — see page 2
2 — see page 3 (top)
3 — see page 3 (bottom)
4 — see back cover
5 — see front cover and pages 5–8

FAIRY 516   433   LST 543
SPUD PIER   BUFFER PONTOON   LANDING SHIP TANK

ABOVE: Representation of LST docking at Susie/Fairy. Another LST, or two smaller LCTs (Landing Craft Tanks), could berth simultaneously on the other side of Susie, but buffer no. 432 is not yet installed.

The Great Storm of 19–21 June 1944

Why, when the moment came, did Mulberry B withstand the shock of the 19–21 June storm, while Mulberry A did not? Mulberry B and Courseulles stand in the lee of both the Calvados shoal to the north-east, and the Le Havre cape. The rocky shoals lent themselves to the specially designed kite anchors (one can be seen at the Vierville museum) which secured the floating roadways, 'trussed up like a woman's corset' it was said at the time. The shifting sands of Omaha provided no such grip, nor was the kite anchoring given sufficient priority. When the storm struck unannounced, it came from the north and north-east, where there were no weather ships, and across a 100-mile (160-km) open fetch of water. The spring tides, combined with low barometric pressure, raised the sea to dangerous levels. Neither harbour had its eastern breakwaters in place and the first contact was with the eastern LST pierheads which were severely damaged by loose craft (see maps and page 16), especially at Vierville. When the surging sea overtopped the Phoenixes there, the 20,000 tons of seawater in each flooded Phoenix had no way of escape as the tide dropped back. Just as they were beginning to burst open under internal stresses eight times their design strength, the Bombardons broke away and advanced on the Phoenix line, adding to the damage. Without the breakwater, the landing craft and pierheads within Mulberry A were at the mercy of the raging sea. At Mulberry B the bulk of the Bombardons ended up west of the port, while the Phoenixes in place were damaged but never submerged (see map).

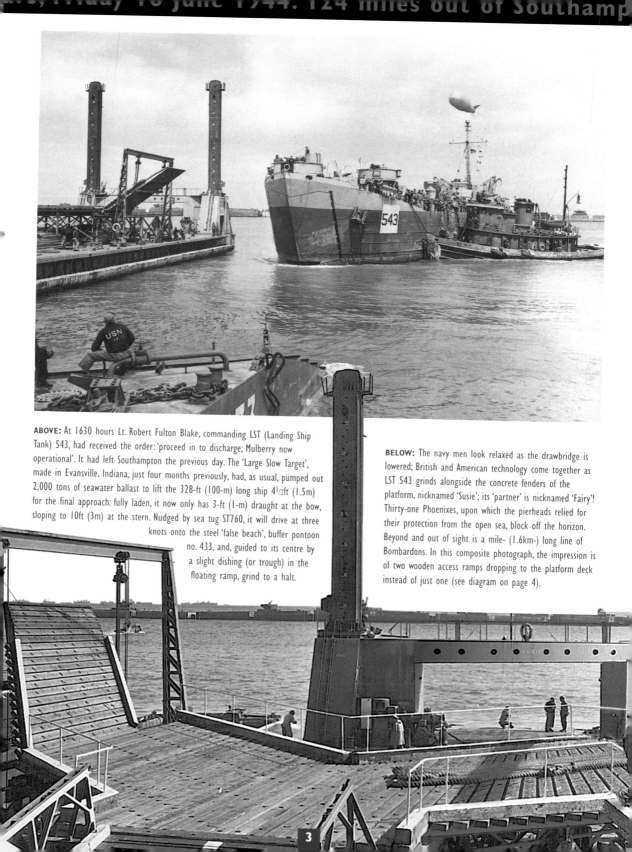

ABOVE: At 1630 hours Lt. Robert Fulton Blake, commanding LST (Landing Ship Tank) 543, had received the order: 'proceed in to discharge; Mulberry now operational'. It had left Southampton the previous day. The 'Large Slow Target', made in Evansville, Indiana, just four months previously, had, as usual, pumped out 2,000 tons of seawater ballast to lift the 328-ft (100-m) long ship 4½ft (1.5m) for the final approach: fully laden, it now only has 3-ft (1-m) draught at the bow, sloping to 10ft (3m) at the stern. Nudged by sea tug ST760, it will drive at three knots onto the steel 'false beach', buffer pontoon no. 433, and, guided to its centre by a slight dishing (or trough) in the floating ramp, grind to a halt.

BELOW: The navy men look relaxed as the drawbridge is lowered; British and American technology come together as LST 543 grinds alongside the concrete fenders of the platform, nicknamed 'Susie'; its 'partner' is nicknamed 'Fairy'! Thirty-one Phoenixes, upon which the pierheads relied for their protection from the open sea, block off the horizon. Beyond and out of sight is a mile- (1.6km-) long line of Bombardons. In this composite photograph, the impression is of two wooden access ramps dropping to the platform deck instead of just one (see diagram on page 4).

The Mulberry Harbours

No harbours – no invasion, and both sides in the conflict knew it. 'Hold the ports and we hold Europe,' declared Adolf Hitler. The Allies agreed: Operation Overlord was not going to be approved without an assurance of Mulberry Harbours.

By March 1943 the pier design had been approved, based upon an old 1923 Lobnitz dredger spotted in Valparaiso by Brigadier Sir Bruce White, in charge of port construction and repairs from 1940, and by June a prototype was being tested in the Solway Firth, Scotland. Nearby, at the Largs conference (2–3 July 1943) convened by Lord Mountbatten in his role as Chief of Combined Services, it was decided to land in Normandy.

In August, the breakwaters were planned: to calm the treacherous Channel waters 56 old merchant ships, four warships, and two Liberty ships would have to be found to form an early, 'self-propelled' screen, scuttled at 2 fathoms (3.7m). Everything else would have to be towed from England. 147 concrete leviathans (Phoenixes) in six different sizes were to be put in place for the two harbours, 60 of them weighing 6,044 tons a-piece, at the 5-fathom (9-m) mark. This would not only allow the steel platforms (spud piers) to operate and Liberty ships of deeper draught to shelter, but would also provide settled waters for an army of craft, such as the hundreds of amphibious trucks (Ducks) and flat flotation rafts (Rhinos) with their tiny freeboards. At 9 fathoms (16m), 93 watertight, but bolted, 300-ton steel cruciform floats (Bombardons) were initially deemed necessary.

An exhausted labour force of 45,000 men was put to work, often in appalling conditions, 20,000 on the Phoenixes alone. It was fortunate that the winter of 1943–44 proved mild for the mixing of 660,000 tons of concrete. It is extraordinary to consider that Phoenix production only began on 31 October 1943; that each pierhead was required to be constructed over a period of four weeks; that the first caisson was under tow on 27 February 1944. It was incredible, too, that two portable ports, each over twice the size of Dover harbour, could be manufactured, gathered, and transported in the largest towing operation in history – all without the Germans guessing their true purpose.

BELOW: It is a beautiful morning, Friday 16 June 1944, Vierville sur Mer. On the first LST pierhead off the Normandy coast an elaborate wooden drawbridge (pages 2 and 3) is being prepared for lowering. Four days later the men of 108th Construction Battalion, known as 'Seabees' ('CBs': marine engineers) would be huddled among the bodies of drowned sailors, lashed to the trembling structure, in fear of their very lives.

The Achievement

At Omaha, the men of the 6th Special Engineers were reduced to slitting open the hulls of stranded merchant ships on the beaches – to find bodies of drowned sailors as well as desperately needed ammunition inside. But even on the worst day of the storm, 21 June, Mulberry A delivered 1,000 tons of ammunition, and Mulberry B 800 tons. Another 6,200 tons of stores came through Arromanches during this three-day crisis. But the storm did no more than interrupt the logistical flow, and the Germans failed to exploit the momentary advantage. The history of the logistics of the Battle of Normandy is almost entirely ephemeral and today there is little to show for it – except our freedom. And yet victory depended upon logistics just as much as upon the fighting man who needed, on average, the support of a ton of supplies every month. By 4 July, the one-millionth man was ashore. Guy Hartcup, the Mulberry historian, wrote: 'Discharge figures for Mulberry B show that by the end of October 25 per cent of stores, 20 per cent of personnel and 15 per cent of vehicles were landed through the artificial harbour.'

We are reminded that the achievement of 1944 was greater than the visible remains offshore suggest. What the harbour provided was the assurance that even in the worst of weathers, reinforcement would continue, as it did during the June storm. It also palpably contributed to the effect of surprise by allowing planners to organize landings on open beaches far from existing ports, in a matter of hours making Hitler's much-vaunted 'Atlantic Wall' redundant. In Churchill's words: 'This miraculous port has made possible the liberation of Europe.'